Money Smarts

Saving Money

by Nadia Higgins

Bullfrog Books

Ideas for Parents and Teachers

Bullfrog Books let children practice reading informational text at the earliest reading levels. Repetition, familiar words, and photo labels support early readers.

Before Reading

- Discuss the cover photo. What does it tell them?

- Look at the picture glossary together. Read and discuss the words.

Read the Book

- "Walk" through the book and look at the photos. Let the child ask questions. Point out the photo labels.

- Read the book to the child, or have him or her read independently.

After Reading

- Prompt the child to think more. Ask: Do you save money? What are you saving it for?

Bullfrog Books are published by Jump!
5357 Penn Avenue South
Minneapolis, MN 55419
www.jumplibrary.com

Library of Congress Cataloging-in-Publication Data

Names: Higgins, Nadia, author.
Title: Saving money / by Nadia Higgins.
Description: Minneapolis, MN : Jump!, Inc., [2018]
Series: Money smarts | Audience: Age: 5–8.
Audience: K to Grade 3. | Includes index.
Identifiers: LCCN 2017027723 (print)
LCCN 2017028559 (ebook)
ISBN 9781624966750 (ebook)
ISBN 9781620318942 (hardcover : alk. paper)
ISBN 9781620318959 (pbk.)
Subjects: LCSH: Finance, Personal—Juvenile literature.
Saving and investment—Juvenile literature.
Classification: LCC HG179 (ebook)
LCC HG179 .H4596 2017 (print) | DDC 332.024—dc23
LC record available at https://lccn.loc.gov/2017027723

Editor: Jenna Trnka
Book Designer: Molly Ballanger
Photo Researcher: Molly Ballanger

Photo Credits: Stephen Coburn/Shutterstock, cover; Derek Hatfield/Shutterstock, 1; Andrei Kobylko/Shutterstock, 3; Donald P. Oehman/Shutterstock, 4 (foreground), Anna Pustynnikova/Shutterstock, 4 (background); Parinyabinsuk/Dreamstime, 5 (foreground); Africa Studio/Shutterstock, 5 (background), 10–11 (background), 13 (bottom), 14–15, 19 (background); Dmitry Maslov/Dreamstime, 6–7; Sergey Novikov/Shutterstock, 8–9, 23bl; RanQuick/Shutterstock, 10–11 (foreground), 23tl; schankz/Shutterstock, 11, 23tl; bluestocking/iStock, 12, 23br; all about people/Shutterstock, 13 (foreground), 19 (left); Room27/Shutterstock, 13 (background); Mark Herreid/Shutterstock, 15; VectorDoc/Shutterstock, 16–17; HomePixel/iStock, 18; Ultrashock/Shutterstock, 19 (right), 23tr; Thomas Northcut/Getty, 20–21; Elena Rostunova/Shutterstock, 22 (foreground); konzeptm/Shutterstock, 22 (background); Kitch Bain/Shutterstock, 24.

Printed in the United States of America at Corporate Graphics in North Mankato, Minnesota.

Table of Contents

Save It!

Tim has money.

What will he do with it?

He will save it!

Tim has a goal.

He wants to
buy a pet fish.

But he does not have
enough money.

Not yet.

He will keep saving.

How does Tim
earn money?

He does chores.

He gets an allowance.

Tim makes
a savings jar.

savings
jar

He draws a picture
of a fish to put by it.

13

He puts his money in the jar.

He will not take it out until he has saved enough.

Save for fish

week 1   week 2   week 3   week 4   week 5

✓				

He checks off a
week on his chart.

After five weeks
he will have enough.

Finally, Tim has enough money saved!

He buys a fish.

He names it Goldy.

Saving is fun.

It helps us buy the things we want.

What will you save for?

Savings Jar

Make your own savings jar to save your money in!

You will need:

- an empty jar
- paper
- a pencil
- tape

Directions:

1. Think of a goal, or what you want to save for.
2. Draw it on your paper.
3. Tape your goal to the jar. It will remind you what you are saving for.
4. Put your money in the jar. Save it until you have enough to buy your goal!

Picture Glossary

allowance
Money earned
for doing chores.

goal
Something to
work toward.

chores
Light jobs
done around
the home.

savings jar
A jar for
storing and
saving money.

Index

To Learn More

Learning more is as easy as 1, 2, 3.

1) Go to www.factsurfer.com

2) Enter "savingmoney" into the search box.

3) Click the "Surf" button to see a list of websites.

With factsurfer.com, finding more information is just a click away.